Mastering Modern Selling Techniques

Strategies, Tactics and Innovations for Thriving in Today's Competitive Marketplace

Williams Dimediator

Table of Contents

Chapter 1

Introduction to Modern Selling

Evolution is the key to success in the ever-changing world of sales. The transition of selling strategies from antiquated, tech-driven approaches to contemporary, modern ways has completely changed the nature of business. Your in-depth guide through this rapidly changing environment is "Mastering Modern Selling Techniques: Strategies, Tactics, and Innovations for Thriving in Today's Competitive Marketplace".

The buyers of today are not just customers; rather, they are knowledgeable, online people looking for individualized experiences and value that goes beyond the sale. Sales tactics must be adjusted in light of this paradigm change. Comprehending this transition is fundamental to contemporary sales, as success is driven by the fusion of human interaction and technical innovation.

This book is your guide through the complex labyrinth of contemporary sales techniques. Each chapter explores a different aspect that is essential for modern sales excellence, from understanding consumer behavior in the digital age to utilizing technology to increase sales productivity. It delves into the skill of telling gripping stories, using social media to engage people, and negotiating the complex world of developing relationships in a digital ecosystem.

This guide is your lighthouse in the constantly changing world of contemporary sales, whether you're an experienced sales professional looking to improve your strategy or an ambitious entrepreneur delving into the complexities of commerce. Accept the change, become an expert in the methods, and prosper in the very competitive market of today.

Chapter 2

Understanding Consumer Behaviour in the Digital Age

Understanding consumer behavior in the digital age is akin to deciphering a multifaceted puzzle, with each piece representing a unique aspect of an individual's interactions, preferences, and decision-making processes. In today's interconnected world, consumers are not only buyers; they are active participants in a dynamic ecosystem of information, communication, and commerce.

The age of unparalleled access to information has been brought about by the digital revolution. With so many tools at their disposal, consumers may now conduct due diligence, evaluate options, and decide wisely before interacting with a company or making a purchase. The significance of comprehending the different touchpoints in a consumer's journey—from first awareness to the last purchase and beyond—has increased as a result of this change.

Moreover, the rise of social media and online communities has amplified the influence of peer recommendations and user-generated content. Consumers often rely on reviews, ratings, and social validation to shape their perceptions and guide their purchasing decisions. As such, businesses must not only understand their target audience but also actively engage with them across these digital platforms to build trust, credibility, and a loyal customer base.

Data analytics and artificial intelligence have emerged as indispensable tools in decoding consumer behavior. By harnessing big data and employing predictive analytics, businesses can gain valuable insights into consumer preferences, patterns, and trends. This enables them to tailor their marketing strategies, personalize experiences, and anticipate customer needs, thereby fostering stronger connections and driving sales.

However, amidst this technological transformation, understanding consumer behavior goes beyond data points and algorithms. It involves empathy, the ability to comprehend emotions, motivations, and aspirations that drive consumer choices. Successful businesses in the digital age blend the power of data-driven insights with human-centric approaches, creating meaningful interactions and memorable experiences that resonate with their audience on a deeper level.

In essence, comprehending consumer behavior in the digital age necessitates a holistic approach that embraces both the quantitative aspects of data analysis and the qualitative dimensions of human psychology and emotion. It's about cultivating a nuanced understanding of the interconnected digital landscape while maintaining a keen focus on the individual behind the screen. Those who master this art are better equipped to navigate the complexities of the modern marketplace, forge lasting relationships, and thrive in an era where consumer empowerment reigns supreme.

Chapter 3

Leveraging Technology for Sales Excellence

In the pursuit of sales excellence, technology stands as both an enabler and a catalyst. Its integration has fundamentally reshaped the sales landscape, offering tools and platforms that amplify efficiency, connectivity, and effectiveness in reaching and engaging customers.

One of the pivotal aspects of leveraging technology for sales excellence lies in streamlining processes. Automation tools, Customer Relationship Management (CRM) systems, and sales enablement software empower sales teams by automating routine tasks, managing leads, and providing valuable insights into customer interactions. These technologies free up valuable time, allowing sales professionals to focus more on building relationships and closing deals.

Furthermore, the advent of Artificial Intelligence (AI) has revolutionized sales strategies. AI-powered predictive analytics helps forecast trends, identify potential leads, and personalize sales approaches based on historical data and consumer behavior patterns. Chatbots and virtual assistants provide immediate responses to customer queries, enhancing engagement and ensuring round-the-clock availability.

The digital era has also ushered in new communication channels. Email marketing, social media platforms, and video conferencing tools offer diverse avenues for engaging prospects and nurturing client relationships. Social selling, for instance, leverages social networks to connect with potential customers, share relevant content, and establish thought leadership within specific industries or niches.

Moreover, technology facilitates data-driven decision-making. Sales professionals can track key performance indicators (KPIs), analyze metrics, and derive actionable insights to refine their strategies continually. Real-time analytics enable agile adjustments to sales approaches, ensuring adaptability in a rapidly evolving marketplace.

Yet, amidst the proliferation of technology, successful sales strategies hinge on maintaining the human touch. While technology optimizes processes and enhances reach, the essence of sales—building trust, understanding needs, and providing value—remains rooted in genuine human interactions. Balancing technology with personalized, empathetic engagement fosters meaningful connections that resonate with customers on a deeper level.

Ultimately, leveraging technology for sales excellence is about harmonizing the efficiency of automation, the precision of data analytics, and the artistry of human connection. The synergy between technological advancements and human expertise paves the way for sales professionals to navigate the complexities of the modern marketplace, surpass targets, and deliver unparalleled value to their customers.

Chapter 4

Building an Effective Sales Strategy

Building an effective sales strategy is essential to long-term success in the cutthroat industry of today. In order to maximize sales potential and match business objectives with consumer wants, a careful blending of strategy, execution, and foresight is required.

A thorough grasp of the target market is essential before developing a strong sales plan. It is possible to determine potential clients' interests, pain areas, and purchase behaviors by carrying out in-depth market research. This information serves as the foundation for customizing goods, services, and sales strategies to successfully address the needs of particular clients.

Establishing precise, quantifiable sales targets is essential. Aim for SMART objectives, which stand for Specific, Measurable, Achievable, Relevant, and Time-bound. Establishing key performance indicators (KPIs) that correspond with these objectives facilitates the monitoring of advancements and the assessment of the efficacy of the approach.

Targeting and segmenting customers are essential elements of a winning sales strategy. Market segmentation into discrete groups according to psychographics, behavior, or demographics enables customized strategies for every segment. By concentrating on the most profitable markets, resources are distributed effectively for optimal effect.

A clearly defined sales procedure must also be included in the strategy. Consistency and efficiency in sales operations are ensured by outlining each stage and putting in place consistent processes, from lead creation to nurturing and conversion. These procedures are made more efficient by integrating a

Customer Relationship Management (CRM) system, which makes lead and customer interaction management easier.

Adaptability should be included in sales methods as well. Being adaptable and quick to modify is crucial in a market that is constantly changing. The strategy's relevance and efficacy are maintained throughout time by ongoing assessment and improvement in response to feedback, market developments, and changing consumer needs.

Moreover, personnel development and empowerment are given top priority in a successful sales strategy. Putting money into coaching, training, and resource provision gives sales teams the know-how and instruments they need to carry out the plan successfully. Creating an environment that values creativity, teamwork, and a customer-focused mindset enhances the effectiveness of the sales force.

Last but not least, a good sales plan requires ongoing performance monitoring and recalibration. Achieving continuous improvement and optimizing performance is made possible by tracking key performance indicators (KPIs), examining sales data, and drawing conclusions from both achievements and failures.

Essentially, developing a successful sales plan requires a comprehensive strategy that incorporates talent development, ongoing assessment, process improvement, goal-setting, market knowledge, and segmentation. In today's competitive business environment, a well-designed strategy not only increases sales but also fosters long-lasting relationships with customers, setting up organizations for long-term growth and success.

Chapter 5

Crafting Compelling Sale Pitches and Presentations

Crafting compelling sales pitches and presentations is an art that involves seamlessly blending persuasive communication, storytelling, and addressing the specific needs and desires of the audience. Here's a breakdown of the essential elements:

1. Know Your Audience: Understanding your audience is crucial. Tailor your pitch to resonate with their needs, pain points, and aspirations. Research their industry, challenges, and preferences to personalize your approach.

2. Start Strong: Begin with a captivating hook—a thought-provoking question, a compelling statistic, or a relatable anecdote. This captures attention and sets the tone for the presentation.

3. Tell a Story: Weave a narrative that engages emotions and paints a vivid picture of how your product or service solves a problem or enhances their lives. Stories create connections and make the content memorable.

4. Highlight Benefits, Not Features: Focus on showcasing the value proposition and benefits your offering brings. Explain how it addresses specific pain points or fulfills desires rather than just listing features.

5. Visual Aids and Simplicity: Utilize visuals effectively but keep the presentation simple and easy to follow. Visual aids, infographics, and concise points help reinforce your message.

6. Demonstrate Proof: Use case studies, testimonials, or data to substantiate your claims. Social proof builds credibility and trust in your offering.

7. Address Objections Proactively: Anticipate potential objections and address them during the presentation. This shows preparedness and instills confidence in your solution.

8. Call to Action: Provide a strong, concluding call to action at the end. Encourage the audience to proceed, be it by setting up a meeting, buying something, or doing more research.

9. Practice and Refinement: Practice your pitch thoroughly. Rehearse delivery, refine content, and seek feedback to enhance the effectiveness of your presentation.

10. Adaptability: Be adaptable to the audience's responses. Listen actively, gauge reactions, and be ready to pivot if needed, ensuring the presentation remains engaging and relevant.

Crafting compelling sales pitches and presentations is about creating an experience that not only informs but also captivates and inspires action. It's a blend of artful storytelling, empathetic understanding, and a clear demonstration of how your offering adds tangible value to your audience's needs.

Chapter 6

Relationship Selling in Digital world

Relationship selling in a digital world harmonizes the age-old principles of building strong, trust-based connections with the technological advancements that define contemporary commerce. It's about leveraging digital tools and platforms to foster and maintain meaningful relationships with customers throughout their journey. This include:

1. Personalization at Scale: Large-scale individualized interactions are made possible by digital tools. Sales personnel may obtain insights into customer preferences, past purchases, and behavior through data analysis and CRM systems, enabling customized, meaningful interactions.

2. Multi-channel Engagement: In the digital sphere, relationship selling goes beyond conventional in-person meetings. Emails, social media, video conversations, and live chat are just a few of the methods it uses to engage with clients.

3. Genuineness and Openness: Establishing trust is still crucial. Even with the digital interface, openness and sincerity in communication are essential to building lasting relationships.

4. Regular and Consistent Communication: Keep in touch with clients on a regular basis. Reaffirm and strengthen the relationship by providing useful information, updates, and tailored messaging.

5. Value-Oriented Approach: Put more of an emphasis on adding value than just closing deals. Genuine concern for the requirements of the consumer is demonstrated by providing pertinent insights, instructive materials, and tailored recommendations.

6. Listening and Reacting: Pay close attention to what customers have to say and answer right away. Make use of feedback systems and social listening technologies to gauge sentiment and modify your strategy accordingly.

7. Customer service and follow-ups: Interactions after the transaction are crucial. In addition to strengthening the relationship, excellent customer service and follow-ups open the door for future recommendations and repeat business.

8. Creating Communities and Advocacy: Establish online communities or forums where clients may communicate, exchange stories, and offer mutual support. Fostering brand advocacy among contented consumers increases the visibility and trustworthiness of your company.

9. Changing Preferences: Remain flexible and adjust to the evolving tastes and actions of your clients. Accept new platforms or technologies that meet the changing needs of your clients.

10. Measuring Relationship Metrics: Track relationship-focused metrics such as customer satisfaction, Net Promoter Score (NPS), and customer lifetime value (CLV) to gauge the performance of relationship-selling initiatives.

Relationship selling in the digital age essentially combines technology and human interaction. The idea is to deliberately use digital technologies to augment real connections rather than to replace them. Through a focus on individualized interaction, establishing credibility, and customer-focused thinking, companies may create long-lasting connections that beyond the boundaries of technology.

Chapter 7

Social Selling: Maximizing Impact through Social Media

Using social media platforms to interact, connect, and develop connections with potential clients has changed the sales environment. This phenomenon is known as social selling. It involves more than just using sales techniques; it also involves building genuine relationships and offering value online.

1. Developing Personal Brands: The first step in social selling is to develop a powerful personal brand. Sales professionals use social media sites like Twitter, LinkedIn, and even industry-specific forums to interact with their audience, offer insightful content, and demonstrate their knowledge.

2. Relationship Building: Direct and genuine communication with prospects and clients is made possible by social media. It's about striking up a discussion, answering questions, and providing answers in a kind, relationship-focused way.

3. Content Sharing and Thought Leadership: Sales professionals can establish themselves as thought leaders in their industry by sharing pertinent and insightful content. It builds credibility and demonstrates knowledge whether it's original material, blogs, articles, or industry news.

4. Targeted Outreach: Leveraging social media's superior targeting capabilities enables sales professionals to reach specific demographics or industries. This focused strategy guarantees that the most pertinent audience is the focus of efforts.

5. Social Listening Tools: Social listening tools facilitate the surveillance of conversations centered around particular keywords or subjects. Comprehending attitudes, worries, and patterns facilitates the customization of strategies and efficient reaction.

6. Storytelling and Engagement: Strong narratives on social media help to break through the clutter. It humanizes the sales process and connects with potential clients to share case studies, testimonials, or success stories.

7. Collaboration and Networking: Social media platforms enable networking with influencers and colleagues in the field in addition to prospective clients. Partnerships and collaborations can increase credibility and visibility.

8. Metrics and Analysis: Monitoring data on engagement rates, social lead conversion rates, and audience demographics can help improve performance and make strategic adjustments.

9. Getting Used to Platform Dynamics: The dynamics of various social media platforms vary. Comprehending these subtleties aids in customizing content and interaction tactics to optimize its effectiveness on every platform.

10. Combining Automation and Personalization: Successful social selling requires keeping a personal touch in interactions, even with the help of automation solutions to help with outreach management and post scheduling.

Building connections and establishing trust online are key components of social selling. If done right, it can result in more enduring relationships, more awareness for the brand, and a continuous flow of quality leads.

Chapter 8

Personal Branding for Sale Professionals

Personal branding has become a powerful tool for sales professionals, enabling them to differentiate themselves, establish credibility, and build lasting connections in the competitive marketplace.

1. Defining Your Brand: Personal branding starts with self-reflection. Identify your strengths, unique value propositions, and the niche you aim to serve. Craft a compelling narrative that reflects your expertise, personality, and values.

2. Consistent Online Presence: Curate a strong online presence across relevant platforms such as LinkedIn, Twitter, or industry forums. Maintain consistency in tone, messaging, and content to establish a recognizable brand image.

3. Content Creation and Sharing: Produce and share valuable content that resonates with your audience. This could include industry insights, tips, success stories, or thought-provoking articles that showcase your expertise and provide value to your network.

4. Engagement and Networking: Actively engage with your audience by participating in discussions, responding to comments, and initiating conversations. Networking with peers, clients, and industry influencers fosters connections and expands your reach.

5. Authenticity and Transparency: Authenticity builds trust. Be genuine in your interactions, share personal insights, and showcase the human side of your professional persona. Transparency in your approach enhances credibility.

6. Thought Leadership: Position yourself as a thought leader by sharing innovative ideas, participating in industry events, speaking engagements, or contributing to relevant publications. This establishes authority within your field.

7. Professional Image and Branding Collaterals:
Pay attention to your professional image—this includes your profile picture, bio, and any branding collaterals. Ensure they convey a consistent and professional message aligned with your brand.

8. Testimonials and Social Proof: Share client testimonials or endorsements. Social proof reinforces your expertise and the value you bring to clients, enhancing your credibility.

9. Continuous Learning and Development: Stay updated with industry trends, technology, and skill advancements. Demonstrating a commitment to learning reflects positively on your brand as a forward-thinking professional.

10. Monitoring and Adapting: Regularly monitor your brand's performance—track engagement, analyze feedback, and adapt your strategy accordingly. Flexibility and adaptability are key in evolving your personal brand.

Building a strong personal brand empowers sales professionals to stand out in a crowded market, establish meaningful connections, and attract opportunities. A well-crafted personal brand not only opens doors but also serves as a testament to your expertise, integrity, and professionalism.

Chapter 9

Overcoming Sales Objections and Closing Deals

It takes skill, insight, and strategic communication to overcome sales obstacles and close deals. It's a delicate ballet.

1. Active Listening and Understanding: It's important to pay attention to the problems that the prospect raises when they object. Prior to coming up with an answer, ascertain the objection's underlying cause.

2. Expect Objections: You can lessen the effect of typical objections by anticipating them and addressing them in your pitch or presentation. This establishes credibility and demonstrates readiness.

3. Validation and Empathy: Show empathy by acknowledging the prospect's worries. Confirm their point of view to show that you understand them before offering a solution.

4. Highlight Value and Benefits: Draw attention to the particular advantages and benefits that your product or service provides in relation to the requirements or worries of the prospect. Pay attention to how your solution addresses their problems.

5. Offer Solutions, Not Arguments: Shift the focus of the conversation away from disagreement and toward providing solutions. Provide solutions or substitutes that directly address the concerns expressed.

6. Employ Case Studies and Examples: You can dispel questions about your offering's efficacy by providing success stories, case studies, or instances of how it assisted clients who were similar to you.

7. Trial or Pilot Programs: By letting the prospect see the benefits directly before committing completely, a trial period or pilot program can help allay concerns.

8. Clarify misconceptions: Sometimes criticisms originate from misconceptions or misinterpretations. To make sure the prospect receives proper information, clear up any misunderstandings.

9. Closing Strategies: Use strategies for closing that are appropriate for the circumstances, such as the summary, urgency, or assumptive close. Select a technique that fits the conversational situation and the prospect's manner.

10. Follow-Up and Persistence: It's crucial to follow up consistently and politely if the deal isn't concluded right away. Success is ultimately possible when perseverance and a value-focused mindset are combined.

11. Learn from Rejections: There is always something to be gained from a rejection or criticism. Examine objections that were raised and modify your approach for upcoming meetings.

It takes a combination of active listening, empathy, persuasive communication, and flexibility to overcome obstacles and close sales. It's about turning objections into opportunities by skillfully addressing worries and persuasively presenting the value proposition of your business.

Chapter 10

Innovations in Sales Automation and AI

Sales automation and Artificial Intelligence (AI) have revolutionized the way sales teams operate, optimizing processes, enhancing productivity, and enabling more personalized and efficient interactions with customers.

1. CRM Systems: These systems, which stand for customer relationship management, automate a number of tasks related to monitoring leads, keeping track of communications, and expediting sales procedures. For the management and analysis of data, they offer a single platform.

2. Predictive analytics: Using artificial intelligence (AI), large-scale statistics are analyzed to predict trends, find possible prospects, and decide on the best sales tactics. Sales teams may now focus their efforts on high-value leads as a result.

3. Chatbots and Virtual Assistants: AI-powered chatbots and virtual assistants respond quickly to consumer inquiries and give round-the-clock assistance. They help human agents by doing basic tasks, arranging appointments, and qualifying leads, thus freeing up their time.

4. Sales For casting and Reporting: Accurate sales estimates and comprehensive reports are produced by AI algorithms that examine past data. This gives companies the ability to proactively modify tactics and make data-driven decisions.

5. Email automation: Leads are nurtured through the sales funnel and engagement is increased via automated email sequences that are tailored based on customer behavior or triggers. They make it possible for focused communication and prompt follow-ups.

6. Sales Enablement Tools: By offering insights into the top-performing content, suggesting pertinent resources, and customizing sales collateral for optimum impact, AI-powered sales enablement tools support sales teams.

7. Lead Qualification and Scoring: Sales teams can concentrate on leads with the highest conversion rates by using AI algorithms to assess and score leads according to a variety of criteria. This improves efficiency and simplifies the sales process.

8. Speech Recognition Technology: By including speech recognition technology into CRM systems, users may enter data without using their hands, take notes while interacting with clients, and update their records quickly, all of which increase workflow efficiency.

9. Social Media Listening and Analysis: Artificial intelligence (AI)-driven technologies examine social media conversations, attitudes, and patterns to offer insightful information for more focused engagement and improved sales tactics.

10. Dynamic Pricing Optimization: To optimize pricing strategies dynamically, artificial intelligence (AI) algorithms examine demand, customer behavior, and market conditions. Revenue is maximized, and competitiveness is improved.

Sales teams can now work more productively, make data-driven decisions, and provide customers with individualized experiences thanks to advancements in sales automation and artificial intelligence. Businesses can increase their competitiveness, expedite procedures, and forge deeper, more meaningful connections with their clients by utilizing these technologies.

Chapter 11

Adapting to Changing Sales Landscapes: Future Trends

Sustaining success in a changing market requires the ability to adjust to the changing sales environments. The following new trends will influence how sales tactics and procedures are developed in the future:

1. Remote and Hybrid Sales Models: Sales procedures have changed as a result of the transition to remote work. Sales teams now need to be skilled at navigating both virtual and in-person encounters thanks to the growing prevalence of hybrid models.

2. AI-Powered Sales Assistants: These artificial intelligence (AI) powered sales assistants are starting to take over mundane chores, provide real-time insights during sales encounters, and automate certain portions of the sales process so that sales representatives may concentrate on higher-value work.

3. Hyper-Personalization: Hyper-personalization in sales is becoming more common as data collecting and AI capabilities improve. Customizing each communication and service to each customer's unique requirements and preferences is quickly becoming the norm.

4. Sustainable and Purpose-Driven Selling: Ethical and sustainable business practices are becoming more and more important to consumers. Sales tactics that highlight purpose-driven projects and corporate social responsibility are more appealing to customers who are socially conscious.

5. Virtual selling and augmented reality (AR): These two marketing strategies provide clients with immersive experiences by enabling them to see goods and services in real time, which improves customer engagement and decision-making.

6. Collaboration across the Sales Ecosystem: In order to deliver smooth customer experiences across the purchasing process, sales teams are working more closely with marketing, customer support, and product development.

7. Data Privacy and Ethics: Sales strategies need to comply with strict data protection standards in light of the growing concerns around data privacy. It is essential to use consumer data ethically and to communicate data practices in a transparent manner.

8. Subscription-Based and Outcome-Based Models: Both outcome-based pricing and subscription-based sales models are becoming more and more popular. Consumers like adaptable, scalable payment plans that reflect the value they obtain.

9. Continuous Remote Training and Skill Development Programs: Continuous remote training and skill development programs are essential for providing sales teams with the changing competencies required in a digitally-first sales environment. This includes remote sales training and skill development.

10. Stress on Emotional Intelligence: As technology becomes more pervasive in sales, it is imperative to emphasize the significance of emotional intelligence in comprehending and establishing human connections with customers.

To stay ahead in a constantly changing sales environment, businesses must embrace technological innovations, adopt a proactive strategy, cultivate agility, and have a customer-centric mindset in order to adapt to these future trends.

Chapter 12

Case Studies: Real-World Applications of Modern Selling Techniques

Case studies are an invaluable resource for showing how modern selling strategies can be successfully applied in real-world situations. They demonstrate how companies have successfully used cutting-edge tactics to produce outstanding sales results:

1. Digital Transformation and Personalized Engagement: A case study could describe a business's journey toward digital transformation and emphasize how they used analytics driven by artificial intelligence to better understand their target audience. They greatly improved conversion rates and client retention by tailoring their marketing with focused campaigns and content.

2. Social Selling and Relationship Building: An excellent case study might show how a sales force used social media channels to interact with potential customers in a genuine way. They increased their network and built trust by exchanging industry ideas, having thoughtful conversations, and cultivating relationships online. This resulted in a marked rise in qualified leads and closed agreements.

3. Innovative Sales Automation: To simplify operations, a business that effectively deployed sales automation solutions could be the subject of a case study. They decreased response times, increased conversions, and enhanced sales efficiency by automating repetitive operations, scoring leads, and optimizing email sequences.

4. Adapting to Shifting Customer Behavior: A case study could demonstrate how a company modified its sales approach to take into account shifting customer preferences. For example, they enhanced consumer engagement and sped up sales cycles by integrating augmented reality (AR) technology into their sales process and offering immersive product experiences.

5. Content Marketing and thinking Leadership: A case study that shows how a business used content marketing to establish itself as a thinking leader may be quite interesting. Their regular production of high-quality content that tackles industry issues helped them gain recognition, expand their following, and improve lead conversion rates.

6. Effective Sales Strategy Pivot: A case study may describe how a company changed its sales approach in the face of difficult circumstances, such as market fluctuations or economic downturns. They were able to weather the storm and develop significantly by focusing on customer-centric solutions, broadening their services, and implementing agile sales techniques.

7. Customer-Centric strategy and Retention: Showcasing a case study that highlights an organization's commitment to a customer-centric strategy could highlight the extra steps they took to meet the demands of its clients. They attained great customer satisfaction with individualized services, reward programs, and outstanding post-sale support, which led to recommendations and repeat business. Case studies are effective instruments for demonstrating the successful use and real-world application of contemporary selling strategies. They provide useful information, lessons discovered, and observable outcomes, inspiring and advising companies looking to improve their sales tactics in the cutthroat business world of today.

Conclusion

The Road Ahead in Modern Sales Success

In the ever-evolving landscape of modern sales, the journey towards success is a dynamic and continuous expedition. As we reflect on the contemporary strategies, technologies, and shifts in consumer behavior, it becomes evident that the road ahead is paved with opportunities for those who embrace change, innovation, and a customer-centric ethos.

The conclusion of this exploration into modern sales success underscores the importance of agility. Businesses must remain adaptable, ready to pivot in response to technological advancements, market trends, and the evolving expectations of their audience. The integration of artificial intelligence, sales automation, and data-driven insights will continue to shape the future of sales, enhancing efficiency and personalization.

Moreover, the human element remains irreplaceable. Amidst the digital transformations and technological innovations, the ability to build genuine connections, understand emotions, and communicate authentically remains paramount. Success in modern sales hinges on striking a harmonious balance between leveraging technology for efficiency and maintaining a human touch for meaningful engagement.

The road ahead also emphasizes the significance of continuous learning. Sales professionals must stay abreast of emerging trends, refine their skill sets, and embrace a mindset of lifelong learning. This adaptability ensures that they not only keep pace with the changing landscape but also stay ahead as industry leaders.

As sustainability and purpose-driven practices gain prominence, businesses that align their sales strategies with ethical considerations and societal values are likely to flourish. Consumers are increasingly drawn to brands that demonstrate a commitment to corporate social responsibility, transparency, and positive social impact.

In conclusion, the road ahead in modern sales success is a journey of innovation, adaptability, and customer-centricity. It is a road where the fusion of cutting-edge technologies with timeless human connection creates a landscape ripe for opportunity. As businesses navigate this path, embracing change and staying attuned to the evolving needs of their audience, they are poised not only to survive but to thrive in the dynamic and competitive world of modern sales.

www.ingramcontent.com/pod-product-compliance
Lightning Source LLC
Chambersburg PA
CBHW070217260726

48658CB00006BA/2107